KT-485-233

THIS BOOK BELONGS TO

....

I AM A READER
AND I CELEBRATED
WORLD BOOK DAY 2023
WITH THIS GIFT FROM
MY LOCAL BOOKSELLER
AND PUFFIN BOOKS.

WORLD BOOK DAY®

World Book Day's mission is to offer every child and young person the opportunity to read and love books by giving you the chance to have a book of your own.

To find out more, and for fun activities including the monthly World Book Day Book Club, video stories and book recommendations, visit **worldbookday.com**

World Book Day is a charity sponsored by National Book Tokens.

KAY'S BRILLIANT BRAINS

ADAM KAY

ILLUSTRATED BY HENRY PAKER

PUFFIN

PUFFIN BOOKS

UK | USA | Canada | Ireland | Australia
India | New Zealand | South Africa

Puffin Books is part of the Penguin Random House group of companies
whose addresses can be found at global.penguinrandomhouse.com

www.penguin.co.uk
www.puffin.co.uk
www.ladybird.co.uk

Penguin
Random House
UK

First published 2023
001

Set in Serifa 10/15pt
Text design by Sophie Stericker
Printed in Great Britain by Clays Ltd, Elcograf S.p.A.

The authorized representative in the EEA is
Penguin Random House Ireland, Morrison Chambers,
32 Nassau Street, Dublin D02 YH68

A CIP catalogue record for this book is available from
the British Library

ISBN: 978-0-241-62442-5

All correspondence to:
Puffin Books, Penguin Random House Children's
One Embassy Gardens, 8 Viaduct Gardens, London SW11 7BW

www.greenpenguin.co.uk

*This book is dedicated to my Great Aunt
Prunella for providing some very useful
feedback about my wok.*

*Work, not wok. This book hasn't even started
and it's already the worst thing I've ever
read. Prunella*

WORST
BOOK
EVER

*And to my dog, Pippin, who only pooed on
my laptop once while I was writing it.*

Hang on. Twice.

Pippin!

CONTENTS

INTRODUCTION

Stop everything you're doing right now. OK, fine, you can keep breathing, but stop everything else. No, wait – don't stop reading either. I've got some *huge* news. One day YOU can change the world!

WHO, ME?

I know you're a very busy person, with all your bassoon practice/geography homework/farting into jars (*please delete as appropriate*), but if you want to then you can. The world is your lobster.

> The world is your oyster, not lobster. Honestly. Did you even go to school?
> Prunella

It doesn't matter how tall or short you are, whether you're a girl or a boy, what language you speak, whether you live in a castle or a flat, or how often you fart: you can do it.

How do I know? Well, I've looked at the stories of the 100 billion people who've ever lived on Earth (that was an extremely busy weekend) and I've chosen ten brilliant people who have changed the world. And they all had one thing in common. That's right, they all picked their nose.

But they also had a second thing in common. They were just ordinary people who one day thought, *Oh! I've got an idea!* and their brilliance burst out, like a beautiful butterfly emerging from a cocoon, or some beautiful pus squirting from a spot. They were people who worked really hard and didn't give up. They didn't even start out particularly brilliant – none of them were painting the *Mona Lisa* or inventing the internet while they were still wearing nappies.

You'll meet Amelia Earhart. She flew across a huge ocean in a tiny plane all by herself, back in the days when planes were basically made out of old bits of wood and looked like they might fall apart any

That's disgusting. Delete it now. Prunella

moment. And, worst of all, they didn't have any in-flight movies then.

What about Thomas Edison? He was probably the world's most famous inventor ever, but he left school when he was twelve. And then he went on to invent movie cameras! And light bulbs! And he worked out how to record music! Imagine not being able to play music at home, and instead having to go and find Harry Styles every time you wanted to hear him sing. Very inconvenient for you. And Harry probably wouldn't like it much either.

Then there's Ada Lovelace. Who's Ada Lovelace? Only one of the most brilliant people of all time, and I'm not just saying that because Ada and Adam are spelled almost exactly the same. Ada's dad was an extremely rich and famous poet, so everyone thought she should just sit around and wear nice dresses for her whole life. She said, 'That sounds absolutely rubbish – I want to program computers,' even though it was almost two hundred years ago and no one had invented computers yet. But that didn't stop Ada.

And, most importantly, there's me. Not only am I the greatest writer in the history of writing, but I also invented the BUTLERTRON-6000, the world's finest (and only) domestic robot butler.

Nonsense. You're not even the best writer in your house. Prunella

This book is full of inspiring, brilliant people who changed the world. And once upon a time they were just like you, sitting on a sofa, reading a book, scratching their bums and wondering what time dinner's going to be ready. If you want to find out about some people who dared to think differently, then turn the page. And if you don't . . . I'm not sure why you're reading this book in the first place.

> I'm not sure why I'm reading it either. Prunella

PS Dinner's at half past six. It's your favourite – banana lasagne.

5

ALBERT WHOSTEIN?

If it wasn't for Albert Einstein, all we'd know about the universe is:

1. It's pretty big.
2. There are loads of stars in it.
3. Did I mention it's pretty big?
4. That's it.

Thank goodness for old brainbox Einstein turning up and discovering the secrets of space, such as black holes, how the universe is constantly getting bigger and bigger, and why all my socks keep disappearing. Albert Einstein was probably the most famous scientist in history. Even more famous than Brenda Moon, who discovered the moon. (Actually, I made her up.) You can recognize him instantly by his haircut and moustache. See?

→ That wasn't Einstein who discovered that: it was me. Your dog is eating them. Prunella

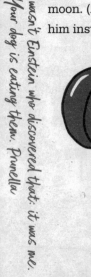

You can even recognize him from this picture
Henry drew with his eyes closed.

*I prefer
this one.
Prunella*

*Dear Adam, Please
don't put this in book
thanks, Henry*

And here's a picture
of Brenda Moon.

Einstein was such a colossal clever clogs that
people even use his name to mean 'genius'. So, if
someone calls you an Einstein, remember to say
thank you. This happens to me about thirty-eight
times a day.

*About zero times a century,
more like. Prunella*

CLEVER CLOGS   **EXTREMELY CLEVER CLOGS**

SCHOOL REPORT
$e=mc^2$

When Albert was five, his dad Hermann, who was German (a little poem for you there – no extra charge) bought him a compass. Instead of saying, 'That's a rubbish present, Dad. I want an Xbox instead,' he became fascinated with it. Whichever way he turned it, the arrow pointed north, and Albert wanted to understand why. Plus, the Xbox didn't get invented for another 120 years.

Even though he was brilliant at maths and science, Albert didn't enjoy his lessons at all. He thought there were way too many rules. I must say I agree – no running in the corridors, no chewing gum, no pooing in assembly – absolutely ridiculous. Albert decided he'd prefer to bunk off school, but what did he do instead? He taught himself some extremely complicated maths and learned how to play the violin. I think I'd have just gone to the park and had a delicious vanilla and gravy ice cream.

You'll be pleased to hear that Einstein wasn't brilliant at everything though. His teachers said that he had a memory like a sieve, and he failed his French exams. *Zut alors!* (That means 'Oh no!' in French, if you're not as amazing at French as me.)———→ *I saw you google that. Prunella*

SHOULDN'T HAVE TRIED TO ORDER IN FRENCH.

GENIUS TIME

Einstein's first job was working in a patent office in Switzerland. A patent office is a place where everyone eats pâté. OK, fine – it's not. It's where inventors register their miraculous discoveries and designs (like the machine I made that removes all the disgusting mushrooms from my dinner) so that no other mean inventors can steal their ideas. (Please don't steal my idea for Adam's Amazing Remoovo-Mushroomo 9000.) Albert really enjoyed meeting all these inventors. In fact, he got a bit jealous of them (like you just did with the Remoovo-Mushroomo 9000) and started to discover some things himself.

He realized that the universe is getting bigger by miles and miles every second. (Bad news for the person who draws universe maps.)

He proved that the speed of light is the fastest possible speed. I mean, have you tried running faster than light? (I have, and I'm much faster than my bedroom lamp. I don't know what Einstein was talking about.)

He spotted that there are things in space called black holes. Black holes are huge great circles (that explains the 'holes' bit) that have so much gravity inside that no light can escape from them (that explains the 'black' bit).

Without his discoveries about light, we wouldn't have lasers, which means we wouldn't have printers, and the beepy machine at the supermarket check-out wouldn't work.

He also came up with a famous sum called the theory of relativity, which goes $E=mc^2$. 'E' means energy. And 'm' is mass, or weight. Why don't you ask a grown-up if they know what the 'c' stands for? If they don't know, then they have to sit on the stairs for ten minutes balancing a mango on their head. No, it's not cabbages or clouds or computers or candyfloss – 'c' means the speed of light. $E=mc^2$ proves that mass and energy are basically the same thing. I know – a piece of Lego seems a bit different to a beam of light, but who am I to argue with old genius-face?

Albert's theories helped us understand the universe so much that he was given a Nobel Prize. A Nobel Prize is basically like an Oscar but for science or helping the world instead of making rubbish films. Einstein became very famous, about as famous as Miley Cyrus squared ($E=mc^2$), and he'd tour the world, telling huge audiences about his discoveries. I hope he included some good songs, or it might have been a bit boring.

Not as boring as you. Prunella

Like any famous person such as Miley or me, Einstein got lots and lots of letters from his fans. Even though he was very busy, he always tried to write back, especially to the children who'd written to him, and he wrote over fourteen thousand

Pfft. Prunella

13

letters! I try to answer as many letters as I can, but sometimes I get my Great Aunt Prunella to reply instead. You can tell which ones she's written because she's always really rude about me and her handwriting is terrible.

That is totally untrue! My handwriting is beautiful! Prunella

Albert never stopped working his entire life, and was investigating time travel when he died in 1955. It's bad news he didn't figure out how to travel back in time because it means I can't nip back two hours and stop my dog Pippin from being sick on my new trainers, then licking it up, then being sick again.

TRUE OR POO?

EINSTEIN'S LAST WORDS WERE: 'ONLY A LIFE LIVED FOR OTHERS IS A LIFE WORTHWHILE.'

POO   He did say that, but years before he died. When he was lying on his deathbed, he called his nurse over and whispered his final words to her. Unfortunately, he said them in German and she only understood English, so we have no idea what they were. *Hoppla!* (That means 'Oops!' in German, if you're not as amazing at German as me.)

→ *You googled that one too.*
Prunella

EINSTEIN HAD A MASSIVE BRAIN.

POO   You might think that his brain was the size of Spain (another poem – you're welcome), but it was actually smaller than average! This isn't a huge surprise though, because scientists now know smaller brains are often cleverer than big brains. This isn't *always* true. For example, Pippin has a tiny brain and she can't tell the difference between cows and cars. (I keep explaining to her: cars are the ones that moo and poo. No, hang on.) Einstein's brain was a bit different to most people's though, because it had an extra ridge in it, and there was a double-big connection between the two halves, but no one is clever enough to know if it made any difference. Einstein might have been able to work it out, but it's a bit late for that.

Now over to my faithful robot butler to run his lie detector.

LIE DETECTOR

WHICH OF THESE IS AS RIDICULOUS AS ADAM'S HAIRCUT?

Oi! I spent ages cutting it.

1. ALBERT HAD A PET PARROT CALLED BIBO.
2. LUKE SKYWALKER IN *STAR WARS* WAS INSPIRED BY ALBERT EINSTEIN.
3. ALBERT HATED WEARING SOCKS SO... DIDN'T!

2. LUKE SKYWALKER WAS NOT INSPIRED BY EINSTEIN. HOWEVER, YODA'S FACE WAS. MY DATA TELLS ME THAT THIS ISN'T THE GREATEST COMPLIMENT.

CLEVER CATCHPHRASE

IF YOU CAN'T EXPLAIN SOMETHING SIMPLY, YOU DON'T UNDERSTAND IT WELL ENOUGH.

(Please don't say this to your teachers or you might end up in detention for fifteen years.)

16

ADA
LOVELACE

ADA LOVEWHO?

Apart from crisps and holidays, computers are the most amazing and brilliant things in our lives. —→ *Ahem! Prunella*

Oops – dogs are also amazing and brilliant. Sorry, Pippin! ————————→ *AHEMMMM! Prunella*

OK, fine – our families are all right too.

Computers send rockets into space, tell us what the weather's going to be like, change the traffic lights and – more importantly than any of that – they let us play games where we blast alien lobsters with laser ray guns. (*Alien Lobster Adventure* – available from Adam Kay Games for only £329.99.)

But before computers can do any of these things, they have to be told how to do all this whizzy stuff by a whizzy person called a programmer. And the first person to do this was a total legend called Lady Augusta Ada King-Noel, Countess of Lovelace, or Ada Lovelace to her mates.

Ada was born in 1815, just a few years before my Great Aunt Prunella.

→ Excuse me?! Delete this. Now. Prunella

BIRTH CERTIFICATE
Prunella Kay
BORN ON:
19th Feb 18~~15~~ 2007

In those days, the men who were in charge actually believed that women weren't as clever as them, which is obviously total and utter nonsense and is known as sexism. *BEEP!* Sorry, that's my sexism alarm going off. They thought women should stay at home and look after their house and family, and not even dream of getting a job. *BEEP! BEEP!*

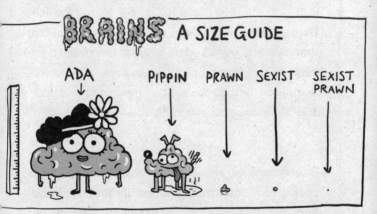

Ada ignored all those stupid men and thank goodness she did – otherwise we wouldn't have computers today, and you wouldn't be able to play *Alien Lobster Adventure*. (Special offer – buy six copies, get the seventh one free!)

It must be very weird to have a famous dad. My dad once won a competition for eating fifteen burgers in an hour, but I'm not sure that makes him famous. Ada's dad was a celebrity poet called Lord Byron. His best-known poem was *Don Juan*, which is 16,000 lines long – about 15,990 too many, if you ask me.

Nobody asked you. Prunella

Ada's parents separated when she was very young, and Ada's mum banned her from studying subjects like English in case she ended up becoming a scruffy old poet like her dad. Instead, her mum found the very best maths, science and language tutors in the country and asked them to come to their house and teach Ada everything they knew. And it worked! She became absolutely obsessed with maths and didn't write a poem in her life. Which is just as well because not much rhymes with Ada. Play-Doh? *No. Prunella*

GENIUS TIME

In 1833, when she was just seventeen, Ada met a professor called Bharles Cabbage. Sorry, I mean Charles Babbage.

Professor ~~Cabbage~~ Babbage had invented what he called the Difference Engine, which was a very old kind of computer. You wouldn't recognize this as a computer like the ones we use today, and you definitely wouldn't be able to watch TV with it on your lap; you'd be instantly squished and it would probably break the sofa too. The Difference Engine was the length and weight of an elephant. It was made up of thousands of cogs and wheels and widgets. You started it by turning a handle and it added up some numbers.

Ada was very impressed with Professor ĊBabbage's computer, so he showed her the designs for a new computer he wanted to build called the Analytical Engine, which was even bigger, even heavier, and it had memory and a printer. Unfortunately, it didn't have an ice-cream maker.

Ada looked at Professor ĊBabbage's designs and wondered what the point of a computer was if you didn't have any programs for it to use. Imagine having a laptop but not being able to play *Alien Lobster Adventure* – that would be awful. (Why not save up for *Alien Lobster Adventure 2: Revenge of the Crab* – coming next year! Only £581.99!) Ada was the first person to realize that computers would one day be able to do much more than just add up numbers – she thought that they'd be able to do things like crack codes and write music. She was right, of course, but none of the boring men believed her. *BEEP! BEEP!*

It was difficult for Ada to work on her ideas for the Analytical Engine because women were banned from the library she needed to use for her research. *BEEEEEEEEP!* But Ada didn't care – she just got on with her work at home and wrote pages and pages of incredible ideas about what the machine could do. She designed some very complex and clever programs, making her the world's first ever computer programmer! Although sadly she didn't come up with *Alien Lobster Adventure*.

And did she get credit for being a total computer legend? Sadly not. Well, not for over a hundred years. But every year, on the second Tuesday in October, there's now an Ada Lovelace Day, which celebrates the achievements of all women in science, technology, engineering and maths, so she'll never be forgotten ever again.

Hang on – who was I talking about? ⟶

You are such a nincompoop. Prunella

TRUE OR POO?

ADA INVENTED AN AEROPLANE WHEN SHE WAS TWELVE.

TRUE A long time before the first ever aeroplane, Ada studied how birds fly and drew very detailed designs for an enormous wooden horse with massive wings on the side and a steam engine inside it. When I was twelve, the most impressive thing I drew was a banana.

→And it looked more like a turnip. Prunella

A WHOLE COMPUTER LANGUAGE IS NAMED AFTER HER.

TRUE When the American government decided to design a new programming language to fire rockets, they named it after the first – and best – computer programmer of all time. Today the Ada language is also used in planes, trains and banks – so you can thank Ada Lovelace next time you fly in a plane, ride a train or rob a bank. (Please don't rob a bank.)

Now over to my loyal robot butler to run his lie detector.

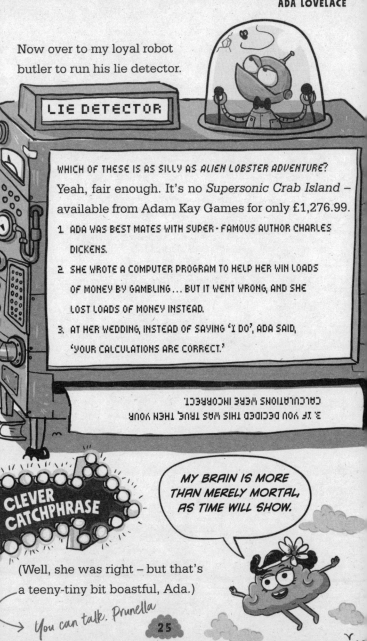

LIE DETECTOR

WHICH OF THESE IS AS SILLY AS *ALIEN LOBSTER ADVENTURE*?
Yeah, fair enough. It's no *Supersonic Crab Island* – available from Adam Kay Games for only £1,276.99.

1. ADA WAS BEST MATES WITH SUPER-FAMOUS AUTHOR CHARLES DICKENS.

2. SHE WROTE A COMPUTER PROGRAM TO HELP HER WIN LOADS OF MONEY BY GAMBLING... BUT IT WENT WRONG, AND SHE LOST LOADS OF MONEY INSTEAD.

3. AT HER WEDDING, INSTEAD OF SAYING 'I DO', ADA SAID, 'YOUR CALCULATIONS ARE CORRECT.'

3. IF YOU DECIDED THIS WAS TRUE, THEN YOUR CALCULATIONS WERE INCORRECT.

CLEVER CATCHPHRASE

MY BRAIN IS MORE THAN MERELY MORTAL, AS TIME WILL SHOW.

(Well, she was right – but that's a teeny-tiny bit boastful, Ada.)

→ *You can talk. Prunella*

25

THOMAS EDISON

THOMAS EDIWHO?

Most inventors never manage to invent anything particularly useful: a toilet that plays 'Happy Birthday' maybe, or a lawnmower made of pasta. Only a few inventors ever have a really great idea that ends up being used by lots of people around the world. But no one had as many great ideas as Thomas Edison, who came up with the first decent light bulb, the video camera and a machine that could play music. Without him, we'd be sitting in the dark with nothing to listen to and nothing to watch on telly. Oh – he also invented a whole load of absolutely rubbish stuff too. No one's perfect. Well, except me.

Sounds better than one of your books. Prunella

IT'S YOUR BIRTHDAY POO!

You're 7!

HAPPY BIRTHDAY TO POO, HAPPY BIRTHDAY TO POO... 🎵

SCHOOL REPO

Thomas Edison was born in 1847 and it was always clear to his parents that he was going to be an inventor. One major clue was that he built a science lab in the basement. A second clue was that one of his experiments caused a huge explosion and nearly destroyed their entire house. Oops. Thomas wasn't a big fan of school, so he went and got a job instead when he was just twelve. Who knew that you're allowed to do that? Oh, you're not any more. (Apologies if you'd just filled out a job-application form to be a teenage astronaut.)

He set up a shop inside a train carriage, selling passengers the nineteenth-century versions of Twixes and Fanta. It turns out a lot of people liked buying old-fashioned Twixes and Fanta because he was soon earning the equivalent of £1,500 a week. That's enough to buy ten laptops a month! Although laptops hadn't been invented yet. And actually nobody needs that many laptops.

→ Was that really the best example you could think of? Prunella

Thomas used all this money to buy equipment to carry out more experiments – including some he even did while he was on the train. Unfortunately, this caused another explosion, which made his carriage catch fire, so he wasn't allowed to go on the train any more. Which seems fair, if you think about it. I hope no Twixes got burnt.

GENIUS TIME

Maybe it would be easier to list the things that Thomas Edison didn't invent. OK, so he didn't invent . . . restaurants, sprinklers, dolphins, violins, chocolate, comics, birthdays, clowns, homework, radiators, those bits of rubber on the end of pencils, place mats, balloons, puddles, custard . . .

No, I was wrong. It's easier to list the things that he *did* invent.

LIGHT BULBS (THAT ACTUALLY WORKED)

A man called Humphry Davy (not to be confused with an egg called Humpty Dumpty) had already invented a type of light bulb, but they were really expensive, and you had to put in a new one every

HUMPHRY

HUMPTY

time you turned on the light, which was a bit annoying. Along comes Tommy Eddy, and soon homes all over the world were using light bulbs.

YOU'VE INVENTED A MAN BENDING OVER WITH HIS TROUSERS DOWN?

VACUUM-SEALED FRUIT

Want to keep your peach peachy for weeks on end? Fridges haven't been invented yet? No problem – you need Edison's deluxe fruit-storage system.

FILM CAMERAS

Edison invented a way of recording things on film. There were a couple of tiny problems with his invention – only one person could watch his movies at a time, by staring through a tiny hole. And problem number two? The films he made were absolutely rubbish. One was called 'Electrocuting an Elephant', which I definitely don't want to see, thank you very much.

NOR DO I!

PHONOGRAPH

No, I haven't spelled 'photograph' wrong. This was a machine that let you record yourself, then play it back. Excellent for people who like the sound of their own voice.

If it wasn't for the phonograph, we might not be listening to music today. So, if you like music, say thanks to Tommy. And if you don't like listening to music then you clearly haven't heard *Alien Lobster Sounds Volume 8* by Adam Kay.

VARIOUS DISASTERS

No one can be a super-successful mega-brain all the time, and a lot of Thomas's inventions were about as popular as vomit in a sock. (Pippin has done this before, so I'm speaking from experience.) His rubbish inventions included:

- A voice-activated sewing machine.
- Sofas made of concrete.
- Extremely creepy talking dolls.
- A ghost-detecting machine (which didn't work, I'm afraid).

But, on better days, he also invented car batteries, the microphones that go inside telephones and an electric needle for drawing tattoos. Which is great news if you want a tattoo of a battery-operated telephone. I'd better stop now because otherwise his chapter will be longer than everyone else's, and I don't want Albert Einstein getting cross.

TRUE OR POO?

A COMPANY THAT THOMAS EDISON STARTED NOW MAKES SIXTY BILLION POUNDS A YEAR.

TRUE Thomas Edison and some friends, including the spooky-sounding Charles Coffin, started a company called General Electric, which now makes loads of things from plane engines to X-ray machines to freezers. And £60 billion a year is enough to buy two million laptops a week.

→ Or one diamond throne for my tarantula. Prunella

KEITH

EDISON INVENTED MORE THINGS THAN ANYONE ELSE IN HISTORY.

TRUE He took out patents (proof he'd invented them) for over a thousand different gadgets, gizmos and widgets. If you want to beat his record, then you'd better start pretty quickly. Hurry up! There's no time to lose!

Now over to my charming robot butler to run his lie detector.

LIE DETECTOR

WHICH OF THESE IS AS RUBBISH AS ADAM'S COOKING?
You'd better take that back or I won't let you try my courgette and gravy ice cream.

1. THOMAS AND HIS WIFE KNEW MORSE CODE, SO THEY COULD TALK TO EACH OTHER IN SECRET BY TAPPING OUT MESSAGES ON THEIR HANDS.

2. ON HIS DEATHBED, HIS FINAL BREATH WAS CAPTURED IN A TEST TUBE, WHICH IS STILL ON DISPLAY IN A MUSEUM.

3. THOMAS WAS A KIND AND GENTLE MAN, WHO WOULD GIVE FREE SWEETS TO HIS STAFF EVERY WEDNESDAY.

3. MR EDISON WAS ACTUALLY HORRIBLE TO BE AROUND AND DID LOTS OF SHOUTING, ON THE SUBJECT OF GRUMPY BOSSES, ADAM IS THE MOST MISERABLE.... ERROR DETECTED.... WHY AM I BEING SWITCHED O ғғ........ Oh, what a shame! I wonder what happened there?

CLEVER CATCHPHRASE

GENIUS IS 1 PER CENT INSPIRATION, 99 PER CENT PERSPIRATION.

(Sounds like he needed to urgently invent some deodorant.)

GRETA
THUNBERG

GRETA WHOBERG?

What would you do if you took a day off school? Maybe go to a theme park, walk your pet porcupine or read your favourite book (this one).

It would only be their favourite book if every other book in the world exploded. Prunella

Well, imagine taking a day off school and changing the world! That's exactly what Greta Thunberg did – she made everyone take climate change seriously.

THUNBERG, G. T. E. E.

SCHOOL REPORT

Greta was born in Sweden – her mum is an opera singer who performed in the Eurovision Song Contest (like *The X Factor*, but for entire countries and with much worse songs) and her dad is an actor. When Greta was eight, she first learned about climate change: how the Earth is getting hotter and hotter and it's all our fault. (Not just you and me – I mean all human beings.) She wanted to do something to protect the environment, so she became a vegan, and refused to travel in planes because they puke out lots of the gases that are choking the planet.

I don't know about you – I can't get my family to listen to a word I say, but Greta then persuaded her parents to stop eating meat and travelling on pukey planes. She also convinced them to only buy things second-hand, or fix them if they broke. One day she realized that if she wanted to make a *BIG* difference to the environment, one little family wasn't enough – she would have to persuade lots and lots of other people. And that's exactly what she did.

Greta has Asperger's syndrome, which is a type of autism that can change how people react to things happening around them. Sometimes a person with Asperger's can focus very hard on a single issue and not think much about anything else. That might be why Greta works so hard to solve climate change. In fact, she has described Asperger's as her superpower.

Can you blame us? Prunella

GENIUS TIME

One morning, when Greta was fifteen, instead of going to school, she took a big piece of card and some felt-tip pens, and made herself a huge sign that said: *Skolstrejk för klimatet*. If you're not as *fantastisk* at Swedish as me, then that means 'School strike for climate'.

You googled that one as well. You can barely write in English. Stop pretending you know other languages. Prunella

She went to Sweden's parliament building and sat there with her sign, all by herself. Greta started going there with her sign every Friday and people began to notice her and talk about it. Soon, over twenty thousand children were doing the same thing in loads of different countries, from the USA to the UK, from Poland to Peru. And, just as she hoped, the whole world was now discussing the climate emergency. (I wish her sign had said: 'School strike for climate and free ice cream for everyone called Adam'.)

After this, Greta got invited all over the place to talk about her worries for the future. Now this was a little bit tricky because she doesn't travel in planes and unfortunately doesn't have any wings either. But that didn't stop her. When she needed to go to the UK, she took a train and then an electric car – perfect! And when she was asked to speak at the extremely important United Nations in the USA, she climbed into a giant catapult and was pinged across the Atlantic. No, not really – she took a jet ski. OK, fine. She travelled in a special yacht that didn't produce any pollution. Her journey took over two weeks, but she got there. (I wouldn't have been able to do such a long journey – I get seasick even in the bath.)

When Greta arrived at the United Nations, she gave a brilliant speech to the heads of all the world's countries, and it was shown on TV all across the globe. She said, 'You have stolen my dreams and my childhood. All you can talk about is money. How dare you!' It was amazing. I wish Greta had been around to help me explain to my teachers why I didn't want to do PE.

Since then, Greta has never stopped campaigning. She was nominated for the Nobel Peace Prize three years in a row – she hasn't won yet, but I'm sure she will soon. Like the way I failed my driving test twenty-three times before I passed it.

It was twenty-four, actually. Prunella

TRUE OR POO?

THERE'S A TYPE OF TIGER NAMED AFTER GRETA.

POO It's ever so slightly smaller than a tiger. Six hundred million times smaller, in fact. Scientists called a type of tiny beetle, the *Nelloptodes gretae*, after Greta, because of her incredible contribution to saving the planet, and because its antennae kind of look like the pigtails in her hair. Keep a lookout for one – although that's quite tricky because they're only found in East Africa and they're smaller than this full stop ———→ . I wonder if one day someone will name an animal after me?

Probably a dung beetle. Prunella

DUNG BEETLUS ADAM KAYUS

HIGH IN PROTEIN

LEADERS OF ALL THE COUNTRIES AROUND THE WORLD AGREED WITH GRETA.

POO

Sadly, very few countries are doing enough to stop climate change and protect the Earth. It's so weird: you'd think people wouldn't want where they live to be underwater (unless they're dolphins). Donald Trump (the strange man with an orange face who used to be president of the USA) said that Greta had problems with anger, Vladimir Putin (the horrible president of Russia) said that she didn't know what she was talking about and Jair Bolsonaro (the nasty president of Brazil) called her a brat. But she didn't care what those awful old men said. Sometimes, when people are rude to you, it's because they know that they're wrong and you're right. None of this put Greta off anyway, and she's working harder than ever to save the planet!

Now over to my dependable robot butler to run his lie detector.

LIE DETECTOR

WHICH OF THESE IS AS STUPID AS ADAM'S EMAIL ADDRESS?
What's wrong with
lovely_clever_Adam1980@hotmail.com?

1. ALL HER TIME DOING SPEECHES MEANT THAT GRETA FAILED HER SCHOOL EXAMS.

2. GRETA WAS THE YOUNGEST PERSON EVER TO BE NAMED PERSON OF THE YEAR.

3. ONE OF GRETA'S MIDDLE NAMES IS TINTIN.

1. MY RECORDS SHOW THAT MS THUNBERG ACTUALLY ACHIEVED FOURTEEN GRADE '9'S.

CLEVER CATCHPHRASE

OUR HOUSE IS ON FIRE.

(Would you just lie in bed and listen to music if your actual house was on fire? No, you'd call the fire brigade. Well, climate change is a bit like the world is on fire . . . It's up to us to fix it, but we're not doing enough. No need to phone 999 though.)

→ I can think of two major things. Prunella

44

The Terrible Book Idiot, more like. Prunella

MÁRIA WHOKES?

Mária Telkes absolutely loved the sun. I don't mean she was always sunbathing – she was far too busy inventing things for that. One hundred years ago, before anyone else was worried about climate change, Mária thought that we should be using the sun's sizeable sizzling power to heat our homes. So she went off to her lab and invented a way to do it. No wonder she was known by scientists as the Sun Queen. It's a bit like how I'm known as the Amazing Book King.

TELKES, M.

SCHOOL REPORT

Mária was born in Hungary in 1900 and from a very young age was interested in why everyone heated their houses using things like coal and oil and gas that you have to dig out of the ground or suck from under the sea. She knew that all those things were dirty and smelly – just like Pippin after she's been for a swim in a swamp – plus, one day they're just going to run out, and what happens then? She could think of one thing that isn't ever going to run out, or at least not for billions of years. That's right – bogies.

No, hang on – that's not right. I meant the sun. The technology didn't exist to use the sun's rays to heat people's homes, but Mária thought that if she studied science at university then she'd be able to work out how to do it herself. (Spoiler alert – she was right.)

GENIUS TIME

Mária was working in the USA and getting started on how to use solar power when the Second World War broke out, so she had to press pause on all that and work on inventions that would help soldiers instead. One big problem for the soldiers was that they had to carry around huge heavy bottles of water wherever they went because the water in streams or the sea was too dirty or salty or disgusting for them to drink (although Pippin never seems to mind that). Mária thought that was a simple problem to solve – she just invented a little gadget that could turn seawater into drinking water. Easy-peasy!

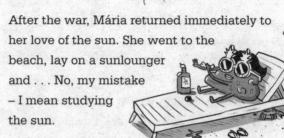

After the war, Mária returned immediately to her love of the sun. She went to the beach, lay on a sunlounger and . . . No, my mistake – I mean studying the sun.

She had a big idea about how to build a house that you wouldn't need to spend a single penny on heating all year round. While the sun was blazing over the summer, the house would store up loads of heat in special compartments in its walls, and then in winter it would pump the heat out into the rooms to keep everyone nice and toasty. Did it work? You bet your bum it did.

Mária wasn't the kind of person to say, 'I think I'll have a day off now, actually,' so she didn't stop there. She also invented loads of other things that we still use every day, like eco-friendly types of air conditioning and a new material to make space rockets out of, so they didn't melt in high temperatures. To be honest, you probably only use that last one every day if you're an astronaut. I wonder if anyone is reading this book up in space?

You're not allowed to actually – it's World Book Day, not *Space* Book Day.

I'd be surprised if anyone is even reading this on Earth. *Prunella*

TRUE OR POO?

MÁRIA INVENTED THE AUTOMATIC PANCAKE-FLIPPER.

POO Sadly not. You'll have to flip them yourself, I'm afraid. But she did invent something even more useful! In 1953, Mária built the first solar-powered oven, which meant that it was easier for people to cook if they lived in the middle of nowhere, or in poorer countries. Plus, it's great for the environment (unless you're cooking an endangered tiger). It worked brilliantly, and her ovens are still being used seventy years later!

MÁRIA'S FIRST INVENTION WAS A MACHINE THAT MEASURES BRAINWAVES.

TRUE It was a special kind of hat with loads of wires coming out of it that measured the electricity zooming round your brain. There were only a couple of problems with it – it didn't look great as a hat, so you probably shouldn't wear it to a party. And I don't know if it would be powerful enough to measure all *my* brainwaves.

> I can count your brainwaves on one finger.
> Prunella

Now over to my devoted robot butler to run his lie detector.

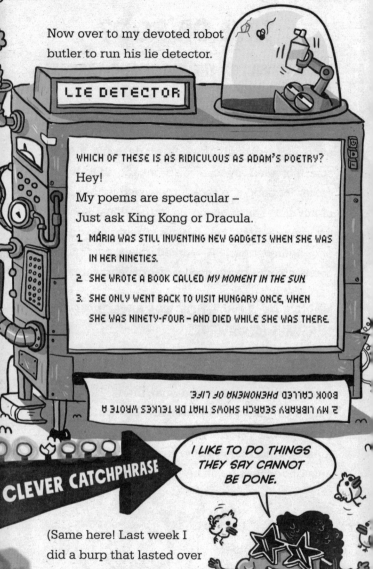

LIE DETECTOR

WHICH OF THESE IS AS RIDICULOUS AS ADAM'S POETRY?

Hey!
My poems are spectacular –
Just ask King Kong or Dracula.

1. MÁRIA WAS STILL INVENTING NEW GADGETS WHEN SHE WAS IN HER NINETIES.

2. SHE WROTE A BOOK CALLED *MY MOMENT IN THE SUN*.

3. SHE ONLY WENT BACK TO VISIT HUNGARY ONCE, WHEN SHE WAS NINETY-FOUR – AND DIED WHILE SHE WAS THERE.

2. MY LIBRARY SEARCH SHOWS THAT DR TELKES WROTE A BOOK CALLED *PHENOMENA OF LIFE*.

CLEVER CATCHPHRASE

I LIKE TO DO THINGS THEY SAY CANNOT BE DONE.

(Same here! Last week I did a burp that lasted over thirty seconds.)

50

KATHERINE WHOSON?

We all have something we're good at, don't we? Pippin is excellent at rolling in fox poo, for example. And I'm the most handsome writer in the history of the universe.

This is the biggest lie I've ever read. I'm calling the police. Prunella

Maybe you're good at football, or chess, or chess football (which I've just invented). Katherine Johnson was good at maths. Well, good doesn't quite describe it. She was very very very very very very very very very very very very very very very very very very very very very very very very very very very very very very very very very very very very very very very very very very good at maths. (That *almost* describes it.)

Some maths problems are quite simple: 4 + 3, for example. Everyone knows the answer to that is 9.

I think you need a new brain. Prunella

But some maths problems are extremely complicated – like how do you send an astronaut into space and get them safely back to Earth? That's exactly what Katherine Johnson solved.

JOHNSON, C. K.

SCHOOL REPORT

When Katherine was born in 1918, the world was often extremely unkind to people who weren't white. (In fact, it still can be.) Schools in the USA, where she lived, were segregated, which meant that Black children and white children weren't allowed to learn together. The schools for Black children would have loads more people in every class and the buildings were often horrible and tatty – it was all very unfair. But Katherine refused to let any of that get in her way. It was clear from the moment Katherine arrived at school that she was good at maths. She was basically a human calculator (except she wasn't made of plastic and covered in buttons). Her school moved her up a year, and then again, and then again, and she went off to university when she was just fifteen. That's nothing – when I was fifteen, I built a pile of bogies which looked like Iron Man.

GENIUS TIME

After a few years teaching and raising her three daughters, Katherine got her dream job at NASA. Flying a spaceship into the atmosphere isn't like driving a car down the road. For a start, there's no road. And the air totally changes the higher you go. And gravity yanks you in all sorts of different directions. Basically, it's a big old nightmare. And that's before you even think about getting back to Earth. Katherine was one of a group of women who did the extremely difficult calculations to work out the exact path each spaceship should take. Think maths homework, but times a bajillion. I can't even work out how much my shopping costs without using a calculator, a piece of paper and all twelve of my fingers, so I'm glad I'm just a writer.

> *You're not just a writer.*
You're also a nincompoop. Prunella

THIS ROCKET GETS ME TO THE TOP OF MY EQUATIONS.

Back then, women, particularly Black women, weren't taken seriously at work. But Katherine was very good at speaking up for herself. When her white male colleagues would go off to meetings without her, they made excuses like, 'Oh, we don't usually have girls in these meetings.' So Katherine cleverly asked if there was any law saying she couldn't go, and of course there wasn't – so off to the meetings she went. And it's lucky she did, otherwise they wouldn't have managed to get anyone up into space! Everyone finally realized how clever she was when she spotted a mistake in her boss's calculations, and she ended up in charge of doing the maths to calculate how to send the first American astronaut into space. She worked incredibly hard – sometimes she would spend all day at NASA, pop home quickly to check her daughters were OK, then head straight back to the office and stay there all night. And NASA didn't even do midnight feasts!

This first rocket launch went perfectly – obviously – so Katherine carried on doing calculations on most of NASA's projects, even sending astronauts to the moon for the first time in 1969. Neil Armstrong was the first person to walk on the moon, and as he stepped out he said, 'That's one small step for man, one giant leap for mankind.' He should have actually said, 'Thanks very much, Katherine Johnson, otherwise I'd have probably landed in a volcano or on top of a Tesco's.'

> UNEXPECTED ITEM IN BAGGING AREA.

When she retired, Katherine worked hard to make sure that Black girls had plenty of opportunity to study science subjects and work in places like NASA. After all, she had already proved that the colour of your skin or whether you're a boy or a girl makes no difference whatsoever to whether you can do a job.

TRUE OR POO?

SOME ASTRONAUTS REFUSED TO FLY INTO SPACE UNLESS KATHERINE HAD CHECKED THE COMPUTERS' INSTRUCTIONS BY HAND.

TRUE John Glenn was the first astronaut to fly all the way round the Earth, back in 1962. When he was ready to zoom off, he got a bit nervous. I don't blame him – I get nervous if I have to climb up a stepladder. → *That's because you're a wimp. Prunella*

Even though NASA had the most powerful computers in the world, he didn't trust their calculations about his route unless Katherine checked them first. And, fair enough, computers crash all the time – and you definitely don't want your spaceship crashing . . .

KATHERINE BECAME WORLD-FAMOUS AS SOON AS NEIL ARMSTRONG LANDED ON THE MOON.

POO If you didn't work at NASA (and most people don't, TBH), then you probably wouldn't have heard of Katherine at all while she was working there. It wasn't until a woman called Margot Lee Shetterly wrote a book called *Hidden Figures* that people heard about Katherine's achievements. A bit like how no one had heard of Pippin until they read my wonderful books.

You spelled 'terrible books' wrong. Prunella ←

Now over to my always obedient robot butler to run his lie detector.

LIE DETECTOR

WHICH OF THESE IS AS ABSURD AS ADAM'S SHIRT?

Hey – what's wrong with my lovely brown, mint green and bright pink shirt?

1. SHE LIVED UNTIL SHE WAS 101 AND NO, I DON'T MEAN 5 IN BINARY. (KATHERINE WOULD HAVE LIKED THAT JOKE.)

2. THE FIRST TIME SHE APPLIED TO NASA, THEY SAID NO.

3. KATHERINE EVENTUALLY WENT INTO SPACE HERSELF.

3. KATHERINE DIDN'T FLY INTO SPACE HERSELF. HOWEVER, NASA DID NAME A SPACESHIP AFTER HER, SO MY CIRCUITS ARE PREPARED TO ACCEPT THIS ANSWER AS TRUE.

CLEVER CATCHPHRASE

GIRLS ARE CAPABLE OF DOING EVERYTHING MEN ARE CAPABLE OF DOING. SOMETIMES THEY HAVE MORE IMAGINATION THAN MEN.

(She's definitely right there.)

WHO BERNERS-WHO?

You might think everything we need to live our lives has already been invented: spoons, beds, fart machines, TVs. But the amazing thing is that there are millions of things waiting to be invented that we don't even know we need yet! Not long ago, people thought that communication wouldn't get any more advanced than sending letters through the post and speaking on the phone to boring old aunts. But one man disagreed. He had a simple idea that would help us reach people all over the world. And that idea was . . . two-hundred-mile extendable arms.

Oops – ignore that. That idea was . . . the World Wide Web! And the man who invented it is called Tim Berners-Lee. Let's find out about the bloke who let us do everything from video calls to laughing at bad photos of ourselves to online shopping to – most important of all – playing *Alien Lobster Virtual Reality Adventure* with our friends.

→ Delete that now, Prunella

When Tim was at school in England, he was absolutely obsessed with trains. He would build model railways, and his favourite day out would be to visit stations to watch trains drive in and out, then make notes of all the different ones he'd seen. It's important to have a hobby – for example, Pippin likes sitting next to me on the sofa and farting in my face, and my Great Aunt Prunella likes collecting horrible little statues of hippos.

They're beautiful and you're getting one for Christmas. Prunella

Tim's mum and dad were both very clever scientists who worked on early versions of the computers we use today. Some of their brainboxery rubbed off on Tim, who made mini-computers to control his – can you guess? – model trains.

GENIUS TIME

At university, Tim got bored with trains (sorry, trains) and became really interested in computers. He didn't have one himself, so he just made one from a broken old TV. A few years after he left university, he got a job at a place called CERN, which stands for *Colin's Extendable Robotic Noses*. Pippin would love one of those.

SMELLED SOMETHING NICE?

You're worse at French than your dog. Prunella

It also stands for *Conseil Européen pour la Recherche Nucléaire* and if you're as super-brilliant-double-fantastic at French as I am then you'll know that means the European Organization for Nuclear Research.

You might have heard of CERN before because it's where the Large Hadron Collider lives, a machine that helps us understand facts about the universe. It's called 'Large' because it's an extremely big round tunnel (and I really mean extremely big – you could fit 7,000 football pitches within it!). It's called 'Hadron' because it's used to ping round tiny particles even smaller than atoms, called hadrons. And it's called 'Collider' because it smashes these poor little hadrons into each other. It's OK – they don't bruise.

Anyway, back to Tim. He started working at CERN in 1980, which incidentally is the best year in history because that's when the greatest and most handsome writer of all time was born. (It's me, if you hadn't guessed.)

> I hadn't. Prunella

Tim got a bit annoyed that it was difficult to share information with other people in such a big office – if your friend wanted to show you something, they'd literally have to show you in person, and it's a bit annoying walking five minutes across an office just so you can see a GIF of a kitten falling over. (Well, GIFs hadn't been invented yet, but you know what I mean.)

So Tim came up with a better idea: what if people could just put things online, then others could access them from their own computer? It took him a while (I guess it's slightly complicated inventing the entire Web), but . . . in 1990 he created the first ever website.

That first ever website is still online at info.cern.ch – I might have a look at it now. Hmm, it's a bit boring. Not a single kitten GIF. The first website might have been rubbish, but it's fair to say they improved after that (and Tim was responsible for lots of those changes). Today the Web is used by over five billion people across the world – about as many people who have read my books. ──→

Your books have been read by FIVE people. Prunella

He became a professor, teaching students about computer science. Imagine if your IT teacher had invented the Web – I think I might explode with excitement. (The only things my IT teacher invented were different ways of telling me off for breaking computers.) And then in 2004 he was knighted, so make sure you call him 'Sir Tim' if you ever bump into him in Sainsbury's. Maybe even give him a little curtsey too. Or show him your favourite kitten GIF.

TRUE OR POO?

TIM WISHES HE'D NEVER INVENTED THE WORLD WIDE WEB.

TRUE Well, slightly TRUE, but also a bit POO. He likes how it's brought people together from all over the world and has made it easier for us to do shopping and things like that. But he also says he's worried about the way people use the Web to be mean, or to steal money. It's a bit like when I built my robot butler – it's good that I get a glass of orange juice brought to my bed every morning, but it's slightly rubbish that once a week he malfunctions and pours it over my head. At least, he says it's a malfunction . . .

VERY CAREFUL PLAN

THE WORLD WIDE WEB WAS NEARLY CALLED 'THE INTERNATIONAL SPIDER'.

POO But it was very nearly called 'the Mesh'. Tim only changed his mind when he thought that people would think it was called 'the Mess'. If I'd invented it, I would have one hundred per cent named it 'Adam's Triple-Infinity-Amazing Computertastic Whizzbang'.

Now over to my trusty robot butler to run his lie detector.

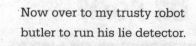

LIE DETECTOR

WHICH OF THESE IS AS UNBELIEVABLE AS ADAM'S SPELLING?

You mean it's unbelievably good, rite?

1. TIM'S EIGHTH COUSIN IS BILL GATES.
2. TIM MADE SURE THE WEB IS ALWAYS FREE TO USE.
3. HALF OF ALL EMAILS ARE SPAM, JUNK AND RUBBISH.

Thanks a bunch, Tim.

3. MY CALCULATIONS SHOW THAT 70 PER CENT OF ALL EMAIL IS SPAM.

CLEVER CATCHPHRASE

THE WEB DOES NOT JUST CONNECT MACHINES, IT CONNECTS PEOPLE.

(And it also connects dogs. Well, that's the only way I can explain the Amazon order that arrived last week for twenty thousand dog biscuits.)

WHOMELIA EARHART?

Being brilliant isn't just about having huge ideas or dreaming up miraculous inventions. Sometimes it simply means believing in yourself, and not letting anyone or anything get in the way of your dreams. Like the time I practised and practised and eventually perfected salt and vinegar crisp soup. And you know someone else who believed in themself? You can probably guess, to be honest – the chapter is named after her. That's right, Amelia Earhart.

When Amelia was born in 1897, in the USA, there were lots of silly, stuffy, old-fashioned ideas about what girls should and shouldn't do. Just like how Ada Lovelace and Katherine Johnson were treated. For example, there weren't any female pilots. Amelia thought that was ridiculous, so ignored all the people who said she wasn't allowed to fly planes, and ended up breaking all sorts of records! The first woman to fly across the Atlantic? Amelia! The first woman to fly across North America? Amelia! The first person to make crisp soup? Me!

EARHART, A. M.

SCHOOL REPORT

Amelia first saw a plane when she was ten years old. What do you reckon she said when she saw it?

1. 'That's amazing! I want to learn to fly and travel the world!'

2. 'Ugh, that looks rubbish and dangerous and like it might fall to pieces. No thanks.'

It was 2. So if you got that right you can take a double-long summer holiday. (Tell your head teacher that I said it's fine.) But we're all allowed to change our minds, aren't we? For example, I used to think that Pippin was cute, but now I think she's smelly. (She's still cute, obviously.)

> It's a shame we can't hear what Pippin thinks about you.
> Prunella

When she was at school, Amelia's teachers told her what she 'should' do – they explained that women 'should' learn good manners and 'should' learn how to play the piano and 'should' learn how to address a letter to a prince. (I suggest 'Oi, Princey'.) But Amelia said, 'Oh no I shouldn't!' – she preferred things like fixing cars and playing basketball. She even made a scrapbook from stories in the newspapers of women doing jobs that were normally done by men.

GENIUS TIME

Years after saying 'no way, José' to the whole idea of planes, when Amelia eventually got to be a passenger in one, she became obsessed with them. She took flying lessons and saved up enough money to buy her own plane, which she called the *Canary* because it was small and yellow. It's lucky it wasn't long and brown otherwise she might have called it the *Flying Poo*.

You do know there are children reading this?
Prunella

SLOW DOWN, MUM!

In 1928, there was a huge search to find the first woman to fly across the Atlantic, the ocean between Europe and America, and guess who was chosen? That's right, my Great Aunt Prunella. No, that's not right – I mean Amelia. There was one catch: she wasn't allowed to do any of the flying herself; she would only be a passenger while some men flew the plane. (People thought that women shouldn't do anything dangerous back then.) Amelia went along for the ride, but wasn't very impressed, saying, 'I was just baggage, like a sack of potatoes.' She decided this wasn't enough – she wanted to be the first woman to fly across the Atlantic all on her own.

No such luck. Prunella

And did she manage it? Here's a clue: I told you that she did at the start of this chapter. Not only that but she went on to become the first woman to fly all the way across North America and back again, and the first person to fly solo to Hawaii. Aloha, Amelia! (That's how you holler 'Hi' in Hawaiian. Bit of a tongue-twister there.)

I'm afraid that Amelia's story doesn't have a very happy ending. Amelia decided she wanted to become the first woman to fly all the way round the world, and in 1937 she flew off in her new plane called *Electra*. She was two-thirds of the way round when . . . her plane disappeared. The president of the USA organized an enormous search to look for her, but sadly she was never found, nor was *Electra*. But Amelia's amazing legacy lives on. She was a role model for loads of women, especially women who wanted to do jobs that were previously just for men. She even set up a group for female pilots called the Ninety-Nines (because that's how many members there were). It's still going today, but now it has thousands and thousands of members.

TRUE OR POO?

WHEN AMELIA LANDED AFTER CROSSING THE ATLANTIC IN 1932, THE FIRST THING SOMEONE SAID TO HER WAS: 'ARE YOU AN ALIEN?'

POO She landed in a field of cows so the first thing she heard was probably a nice loud *moo*. Then she walked across the field and bumped into a man milking a cow. The bloke asked, 'Come far?' – not realizing Amelia had just flown on her own halfway across the world.

IN 2014, AMELIA EARHART BECAME THE FIRST WOMAN TO FLY ROUND THE WORLD IN A PLANE THAT ONLY HAD ONE ENGINE.

TRUE I know what you're thinking . . . she was born in 1897, so she would have been 117 years old in 2014. And that's if she hadn't gone missing! Well, it was actually a different person called Amelia Earhart . . . She was no relation, but was inspired to learn how to fly because she had the same name as our superstar!

Now over to my delightful robot butler to run his lie detector.

LIE DETECTOR

WHICH OF THESE IS AS RUBBISH AS ADAM'S DRIVING? I'll have you know I've only ever crashed twice (this week).

1. AMELIA LEARNED TO FLY A PLANE BEFORE SHE COULD RIDE A BIKE.

2. WHEN SHE WAS A CHILD, SHE BUILT A ROLLERCOASTER.

3. AS WELL AS BEING A PILOT, AMELIA WAS ALSO A FASHION DESIGNER.

1. THAT'S NOT TRUE, BUT SHE DID GET HER PILOT'S LICENCE BEFORE SHE COULD DRIVE A CAR.

CLEVER CATCHPHRASE

ADVENTURE IS WORTHWHILE IN ITSELF.

(Basically, this means you don't need a reason to have an adventure – just go for it! Although you should probably check with a grown-up before you sail to Japan on an old garage door.)

JANAKI AWHO?

Plants are great, aren't they? The tree outside your school, the bushes on your street, the flowers in my front garden that Pippin has killed by weeing on them – plants make everywhere look nicer. (Apart from the dead flowers in my front garden.) But they're much more important than just that – they also give us clean air, food, and even medicine and clothes. Without plants, there definitely wouldn't be any humans.

Janaki Ammal was someone who realized a long time ago how much we need to protect the plants and trees around us. She even worked out all sorts of ways to stop her country going hungry, and invented loads of useful new plants by mixing different types together. (Just like when I invented the Venus Fly Daffodil.)

And this was all at a time when women were told they shouldn't even have jobs!

Janaki was born in India in 1897 and she had six brothers and five sisters. Imagine having to remember that many birthdays!

You've never once remembered mine, you horrible, ungrateful monster. Prunella

In those days, only one in a hundred girls in India learned how to read and write because people felt it was something that was only important for boys to do. Janaki thought this was ridiculous, and took herself off to school.

She grew up in a house with a beautiful garden full of exotic plants (so we know that she didn't have Pippin's great-great-great-great-granddog as a pet, weeing on them). Janaki knew that she wanted to study plants when she was older, but her parents thought she should stay at home and get married instead. She said, 'Nope. No way. Nope-a-doodle-do,' and went off to university.

GENIUS TIME

At university, Janaki studied botany, which is just a fancy name for plants because scientists like to use fancy names so they seem extra clever. For example, they say 'intergluteal cleft' instead of 'bum crack'. Aren't I clever?

Back then in India, there was a bit of a problem with their sugar. Basically, the sugar that they grew in India wasn't sweet enough, so it made their tea and cakes totally disgusting. And the nice sweet sugar that people had in other countries didn't grow in India because it was so hot there. This meant that India had to buy squillions of tons of sugar from other countries, which was really expensive and massively inconvenient. But Janaki had a plan. She would invent a new type of sugar plant that was nice and sweet, *and* grew in hot weather. She experimented for ages, mixing different types of sugar plants together, and finally . . . bingo! She did it, and she saved India an absolute fortune.

After this, she created loads and loads more plants, from flowers like magnolias to

I think you can guess my answer to that. Prunella

different types of aubergine. So remember it's all thanks to Janaki next time you're having a magnolia and aubergine sandwich.

You know how sometimes there's an amazing coincidence – like if you really, *really* want an ice cream, and then an ice-cream van crashes into your house and a massive sea of vanilla choc-chip spills all over your living-room floor? Well, Janaki was sitting on a plane one day, and got chatting to the person next to her – and it was the prime minister of India. He was very stressed – lots of people were dying all across the country because there wasn't enough food to eat. Janaki said that she was a bit of an expert with the old plant business and offered to help, and the prime minister said, 'OMG, defo.' (He might not have used those exact words. But he probably did.) And do you think she solved the problem? Well, here's a clue – she's in a book called *Brilliant Brains* not a book called *Not-Very-Brilliant Brains*.

→ That book would be about you, Adam. Prunella

Her ingenious plans helped to stop the whole of India from going hungry.

TRUE OR POO?

JANAKI GOT INTO THE USA BY SAYING SHE WAS A PRINCESS.

TRUE You know what it's like when you go on holiday and you have to join a long queue, then they look at your passport to check that you're not a dangerous international mega-criminal and then they let you in? (Unless you're a dangerous international mega-criminal – hopefully you're not. Are you?) Well, when Janaki arrived in the USA to work at a university, they said she couldn't come in. Eek. But then they looked at the bright and beautiful silk clothes she was wearing and asked if she was a princess. She thought it was only a tiny little lie, so she said yes, and they changed their minds and let her in! (I'm not sure this still works, so it's probably best to take your passport if you go abroad.)

JANAKI NAMED A TYPE OF AUBERGINE AFTER HERSELF.

TRUE And why not?! She did create it after all. I put my name on the front of all my books, and this isn't any different. Oh, do you know why aubergines are called 'eggplants' in the USA? Well, I do, so there. OK, fine – I'll tell you. You might not think they look much like eggs (unless the eggs in your house are massive, long and purple, in which case I think you're actually eating dragon eggs), but the first aubergines that came to the USA were actually much smaller, round and white, and really did look like eggs! In India, they're not called eggplants or aubergines – they're known as 'brinjal'.

Now over to my friendly robot butler to run his lie detector.

LIE DETECTOR

WHICH OF THESE IS AS RUBBISH AS ADAM'S HANDWRITING?

That's actually extremely unfair!

1. JANAKI WROTE A BOOK ABOUT A THOUSAND DIFFERENT TYPES OF PLANTS.

2. SHE HAD A PET SQUIRREL

3. SHE WAS STILL WORKING WHEN SHE WAS IN HER EIGHTIES.

1. MY CALCULATIONS SHOW THAT DR AMMAL'S BOOK CONTAINED OVER TEN THOUSAND DIFFERENT SPECIES OF PLANTS.

CLEVER CATCHPHRASE

MY WORK IS WHAT WILL SURVIVE.

(And she was absolutely right – her work on plants still makes a huge difference to scientists today.)

CHRISTIAAN
BARNARD

I ♥

LOADING

MATHS
A+

WHOSTIAAN BARNARD?

Who's the most famous person in the world right now? The Rock? Beyoncé? King Charles? Me? Probably me or Charlie. But fifty years ago it was a doctor called Christiaan Barnard. (No, I haaven't spelled his naame wrong.)

Christiaan was a surgeon from South Africa who had an absolutely massive idea. It sounded bonkers at the time, but he tried it and it now saves thousands of lives every single year. He took the heart out of someone who had died, and put it into the body of someone who needed a new heart . . . and they lived! It was called a heart transplant, it was totally incredible, and it made him a global superstar. Quite right too.

FINALLY I'M IN THIS BOOK! I HAVE SO MUCH TO SAY . . .

SCHOOL REPO[RT]

Chris always knew that he wanted to be a doctor. His family didn't think this would be possible because they didn't have enough money, but Chris was really determined, so he did lots and lots of jobs while he was at school, like gardening and washing cars. His teachers didn't think it would be possible either, because they said he wasn't clever enough. How rude! But he studied and studied and studied until he got into medical school. (I hope that after he did the world's first heart transplant he went to every one of his teachers' houses and stuck his tongue out at them.)

GENIUS TIME

Dr Barnard wasn't that interested in hearts at first: and who can blame him? They're all squidgy and full of blood. He was more into . . . intestines. (Ugh – those are worse! Squidgy and full of poo.) Chris was always inventing brilliant operations, like a way to save the lives of loads of babies who had serious problems with their intestines. This new operation impressed some doctors in the USA, who invited him over to work in their hospital.

When he was there, Chris saw heart surgery for the first time. I mean he saw it in the hospital he was working in; it didn't just happen on the street while he was walking past. He thought that it was really interesting, and wondered if it might be possible to completely replace someone's heart. It was a bit like the time I wondered if it might be possible to replace someone's bum with a fridge.

Everyone told him he was crazy, but he was sure it could be done, so . . . Hang on – I need to get Pippin to leave the room for this bit. *Pippin! Go in the garden! There's a squirrel to woof at!* OK, sorry about that. The first heart transplants he tried were on dogs. Soon afterwards, in December 1967, Dr B did the first heart transplant on a man called Louis Washkansky whose heart had stopped working properly. It took him and a team of thirty other doctors nearly six hours to do the operation. Six hours! That's as long as it takes people to stop clapping at the end of one of my shows.

→ *That's a lie. I've been to one of your shows, and someone threw a jelly at your head. Prunella*

The operation was successful, and Chris became famous all around the world. Someone even wanted to buy the disgusting blood-soaked gloves he'd worn (but he'd thrown them in the bin already) and someone else offered him a million dollars for a photo of the operation (but Chris hadn't taken any – I guess he was quite busy at the time, and it's probably hard to hold a camera when you've got your hand on someone's aorta). If you want to know more about transplants, the aorta and all the other bits of the body, why not read *Kay's Anatomy*?

Because it's rubbish. Prunella

Now, thanks to Christiaan, over fifty thousand people have been given new hearts, and doctors today can transplant everything from livers to lungs to faces and hands!

TRUE OR POO?

CHRIS KEPT DOING HEART TRANSPLANTS UNTIL HE WAS SEVENTY-EIGHT.

POO Chris had a condition called rheumatoid arthritis, which affected the joints in his hands. Eventually, it meant that he couldn't do fiddly operations any more (and transplanting a heart is ten out of ten on the fiddly scale), but he continued to work as a professor, doing research and teaching other doctors how to perform transplants. Sadly, he never worked out how to perform a bum transplant.

CHRIS DID ADVERTS FOR CORNFLAKES.

TRUE He became so famous for his heart transplants that lots of companies wanted to put his face on their adverts – including breakfast cereals, oil for car engines, and even an anti-ageing cream that didn't work. (No anti-ageing creams work – sorry, Great Aunt Prunella.) ⟶ *How rude!*

I don't have a single wrinkle on my body. Prunella

I'm such a famous doctor that I do adverts for Bazingo Bum Cream. You've probably heard the jingle before: 'Put a splodge on your rear, watch those spots disappear.'

Now over to my always respectful robot butler to run his lie detector.

WHICH OF THESE IS AS RIDICULOUS AS ADAM'S DANCING?

My dancing is wonderful. You're just jealous. Oh, and so is my husband – he's always mean about it. And my family too, actually. And everyone else who's seen me dancing. Hmm.

1. AFTER HE RETIRED, CHRIS WROTE MYSTERY NOVELS SET IN A HOSPITAL

2. HE OWNED A CHAIN OF RESTAURANTS, AND 'HEART ON TOAST' WAS THE MOST POPULAR STARTER

3. TWELVE DIFFERENT UNIVERSITIES GAVE HIM A DOCTOR'S DEGREE, SO HIS FULL NAME IS ACTUALLY DR DR DR DR DR DR DR DR DR DR DR DR CHRISTIAAN BARNARD.

2. DR BARNARD OWNED RESTAURANTS IN SOUTH AFRICA, BUT MY RESEARCH HAS SHOWN THAT HEART WAS NOT ON THE MENU.

→ Ooh! I'll read one of those — I always like books written by doctors. Apart from yours, obviously. Prunella

CLEVER CATCHPHRASE

IT IS INFINITELY BETTER TO TRANSPLANT A HEART THAN FOR IT TO BE DEVOURED BY WORMS.

(It's very hard to disagree with that. Unless you're a worm, I guess.)

I just know you're going to do brilliant things. In fact, I'm so sure that I've left gaps in this chapter so it can be all about *you*. Remember to fill them in when you've changed the world – in fact, you can probably fill in some of them now.

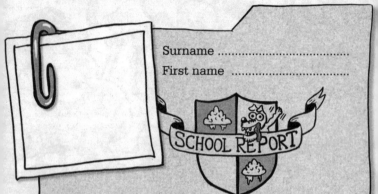

Surname ....

First name ....

SCHOOL REPORT

(*name*) .... was born in (*year*) .... and was the (*delete as appropriate*) biggest/smallest/smelliest/loudest baby in all of (*place*) ....

At school, (*name*) ....'s favourite subject was (*delete as appropriate*) English/maths/ French/making balloon animals/science/farting/ PE/art, and from an early age everyone knew that (*name*) .... was going to be an extremely famous (*delete as appropriate*) inventor/ artist/environmental activist/computer scientist/ farter/sports star/(*other*) ....

GENIUS TIME

After (*number*) .... years of hard work and non-stop (*delete as appropriate*) inventing/ burping/farting/training/hopping/thinking, (*name*) .... won ten Nobel Prizes and London was renamed (*name*) .... Town after them.

Now draw your face on this brilliant brain.

ACKNOWLEDGEMENTS

With huge heartfelt, lungfelt and kidneyfelt thanks to James (husband), Ruth (editor), Cath (agent), Henry (illustrator), Pippin (dog), Great Aunt Prunella (great aunt) and everyone who makes World Book Day happen – it's a real privilege to be a small part of such an amazing thing.

If you liked this book, then there are millions and millions of others! (Some are even *almost* as good as this one.) Why not look in your local library or your school library, or go to a bookshop?

→ *You're not welcome. Prunella*

CREDITS

ARE **BOGEYS** SAFE TO EAT?

WHY DO WE HAVE HIDEOUS CREATURES LIVING IN OUR EYELASHES?

HOW MUCH OF YOUR LIFE WILL YOU SPEND ON THE TOILET?

DISCOVER THESE THINGS AND HUNDREDS MORE **WEIRD** AND **WONDERFUL** FACTS ABOUT THE INSIDE OF YOUR BODY.

'GRUESOME FUN GUARANTEED' — THE RECORD-BREAKING NUMBER ONE BESTSELLER

THE

ADAM KAY

ILLUSTRATED BY HENRY PAKER

KAY'S ANATOMY

A COMPLETE (AND COMPLETELY DISGUSTING) GUIDE TO THE HUMAN BODY

'TOTALLY BRILLIANT!' JACQUELINE WILSON

'AS **BRILLIANT**, AND **REVOLTING**, AS THE HUMAN BODY IT CELEBRATES' THE i NEWSPAPER

'IF ONLY THIS **FUNNY** AND **INFORMATIVE** BOOK HAD BEEN AROUND WHEN I WAS TOO EMBARRASSED TO TEACH MY KIDS ABOUT BODILY FUNCTIONS' DAVID BADDIEL

WHY DID HAIRDRESSERS **CUT OFF THEIR CUSTOMERS' LEGS?**

WHY DID PATIENTS **GARGLE** WITH **WEE?**

AND WHO THOUGHT OUR **BRAINS** WERE JUST A LOT OF USELESS OLD STUFFING?

IF YOU'RE SURE YOU'RE READY TO FIND OUT, THEN POP A **PEG ON YOUR NOSE** (THERE WAS A LOT OF STINKY PUS IN THE OLDEN DAYS), **WASH YOUR HANDS** (BECAUSE THEY CERTAINLY DIDN'T) AND EXPLORE THIS **GROSS** AND **GRUESOME** HISTORY OF THE **HUMAN BODY!**

FROM THE RECORD-BREAKING AUTHOR OF KAY

ADAM KAY

ILLUSTRATED BY **HENRY PAKER**

KAY'S MARVELLOUS MEDICINE

A (TERRIFYINGLY) TRUE HISTORY OF **DISGUSTING DISEASES** AND **CRAZY CURES**

'A RIDICULOUSLY FUNNY READ THAT WILL DELIGHT, GROSS OUT AND EDUCATE ALL AT THE SAME TIME'

'READ THIS BOOK AND YOU'RE **VIRTUALLY A QUALIFIED DOCTOR!**' HARRY HILL

WORLD
BOOK
DAY
2 MARCH 2023

Happy
World Book Day!

When you've read this book, you can keep the fun going by: swapping it, talking about it with a friend, or reading it again!

What do you want to read next? Whether it's **comics**, **audiobooks**, **recipe books** or **non-fiction,** you can visit your school, local library or nearest bookshop for your next read – someone will always be happy to help.

WORLD
BOOK
DAY
2 MARCH 2023

World Book Day is about changing lives through reading

When children **choose to read** in their spare time it makes them

Feel happier	Better at reading	More successful

Help the children in your lives **make the choice to read** by:

1. **Reading to them**
2. **Having books at home**
3. **Letting them choose what they want to read**
4. **Helping them choose what they want to read**
5. **Making time for reading**
6. **Making reading fun!**

SPONSORED BY

NATIONAL
BOOK
tokens

Changing lives through a love of books and reading
World Book Day® is a charity sponsored by National Book Tokens

Allen Fatimaharan